The Num
SAF

Self Awareness Formulas

Kathy M. Scogna
Joseph R. Scogna, Jr.

The Numbers of SAF

Self Awareness Formulas

The Numbers of SAF
by Kathy M. Scogna
Joseph R. Scogna, Jr.

Copyright © 2015 by Kathy M. Scogna
All Rights Reserved.

No part of this book may be reproduced or transmitted in any form or by any means, electronic or mechanical, including photocopying, recording or by any information storage retrieval system without permission of the copyright owner, except for reviews with the proper citation.

wwwKathyScogna.com
Life Energy Publications * www.LifeEnergyResearch.com

Available as a Kindle e-Book

   To the Reader: This work reflects the research of Joseph R. Scogna, Jr. It is not a medical manual nor should it be used to diagnose diseases or prescribe medicine or drugs. It is published for reference and educational purposes so that SAF participants and their practitioners can understand the SAF numbering system.
   The Reader is urged to consider his or her own unique set of circumstances; if disease, poor health, illness or continuing symptoms, however minor, are present, he or she should seek the proper health practitioner of choice. This is a prudent idea before embarking on any nutritional, health, or spiritual endeavor.

Cover design by Kathy M Scogna; number collage on cover by 5abbNumbers-15 13061jpg.

The Numbers of SAF
Includes index
Scogna, Kathy M. author, editor
1.   SAF Numbering System   2. Self Awareness Formulas
3. SAF   4. Holistic Health
I. Kathy M. Scogna author, editor II. Joseph R. Scogna, Jr. author
III. Title

ISBN —13: 978-1516889426
ISBN —10: 1516889428

Contents

Foreword —————————————————— 7
How to Use this Book ——————————— 11
FAQs ——————————————————————— 13
#1 thymus—aggression ————————— 19
#2 heart—synchronize ————————————— 21
#3 colon—detoxify ———————————————— 23
#4 stomach—digestion ————————————— 25
#5 anterior pituitary—coordinate ————— 27
#6 liver—transmutate ————————————— 29
#7 lungs—vaporization ———————————— 31
#8 sex organs—reproduce ——————————— 33
#9 bones/muscles—locomotion ——————— 35
#10 thyroid—metabolization ——————— 37
#11 veins/arteries—circulation ——————— 39
#12 brain/nervous system—electricity ——— 41
#13 adrenal glands—capacitance ————— 43
#14 mind—analyze ————————————————— 45
#15 hypothalamus/senses—evaluation ——— 48
#16 kidneys/bladder—filtration ————— 51
#17/18 endocrine system—equalize ———— 53
#19 skin—demarcate ————————————— 56
#20 pancreas/solar plexus—location ——— 58
#21 posterior pituitary—hydrolyze ——— 61
#22 parathyroid—experience ——————— 63
#23 spleen—rejection ————————————— 65
#24 lymph system/EPF—accept ————— 67
Endocrine Sense Channels (SAF Operative Chart) — 70
Suggested Reading ———————————————— 72
Index ——————————————————————— 73
Words from Happy Clients! ———————— 76
Practitioners Speak ———————————————— 77

Foreword

For at least the last 5,000 years of recorded history, medicine and spirituality have been aligned in Natural Philosophy. While many Asians followed the tenets of Lao Tzu who wrote down the ancient teachings into the *I Ching: The Book of Changes,* the Greeks followed the study of the humors, the progression a disease takes as experienced by symptomatology. In these Natural Philosophies, illness was not considered a specific disease but rather a collection of symptoms brought on by an imbalance. Once this imbalance was corrected, harmony would be restored. The purpose was to bring about harmony and balance, which is how the Asians, Greeks and homeopathic physicians all defined "health."

With the invention of the microscope, the formerly invisible became visible and a new world opened up. A schism then occurred in Natural Philosophy. Medicine and science took a sharp turn on the path to address only what was visible (1% of reality) leaving philosophy and spirituality to grapple with the invisible.

Our base of knowledge is greater today than in the past, but are we smarter than the ancient ones? Of the writings that remain, on cave walls, on papyrus, in books, it would appear we have lost something crucial and dynamic – our propensity and will to know ourselves as a composite of body, mind and spirit.

While the microscope has been justly heralded for its benefits to mankind, it has also led to our downfall as perceptual beings. No longer are we validated or allowed to intuitively know and understand life or explore our spiritual selves. Knowledge must now be <u>seen</u> for it to be true. And that duty of seeing and diagnosing has been relegated to the doctor and lab technician with the microscope.

Our definition of health has changed. Somewhere along the way, we have lost our capacity to understand the invisible, which makes up 99% of existence. We have become obedient patients, patiently waiting for the doctor to give a title to our physical ailment. We are then bombarded with the latest lab-created medicines and approved drugs, many of which are later determined to be deadly, with far more serious side effects than our original complaint.

We rarely hear a word about balance. Anyone who even whispers the word "balance" or "harmony" is often dismissed as a quack, and driven out.

Joseph R. Scogna, Jr. was not one to accept this status quo. He was able to peer down the time track of humanity looking for the energetic solutions to the troubles of man, our symptoms and our imbalances. On this mental trek, Joe took with him an understanding of cosmic and atomic energy (quantum physics) and he applied this to the studies of the past, specifically symptomatology as found in homeopathy, the humors of the Greeks and the balance of the *I Ching*.

Joe used deep and personal philosophical reflection and various modern machines and devices, including computers and infrared, to define the electroplasmic field around living beings (our energy field), and to codify the metabolic connections of body, mind and spirit. He dismissed the word "patient," brought back the word "balance," and has given mankind a modern day Natural Philosophy that incorporates both the visible and the invisible.

The Self Awareness Formulas (SAF) is a practical use of Joe Scogna's published life energy research into symptomatic patterns and our holistic connections. There are books for beginning travelers and experienced self-sojourners. *Nutrionics: Introduction to Elemental Pairs* explains the nature of balance as found in and used by everything on this planet - minerals, plants, animals, humans. *Junk DNA: Unlocking the Hidden Secrets of Your DNA* explains the basis of SAF work, with the 128 perceptions we humans could be using instead of the currently accepted five senses. *Project Isis: Fundamentals of Human Electricity* explains our electrical life force, how SAF fits into the scheme of electrical energy, and how we can use infrared devices to find and utilize this energy to our advantage.

SAF Simplified highlights the language of SAF; it presents theory and an in-depth view of the organs and glands and numbers, with instructions for reading SAF chain sequences. When we understand the language of SAF, we can finally listen to the chatter of our organs and glands and the messages they are sending to us about our symptoms. SAF is the Rosetta Stone, the translator for the body, our symptoms, our past!

SAF Simplified is considered a companion to this book (*The Numbers of SAF*). A fun learning tool to help memorize the numbers and meanings found in this book, can be found in *SAF Flashcards*.

The Numbers of SAF is designed to help those who are on a self-awareness journey, either as beginners or as seasoned travelers, working with practitioners or working alone. This is a journey into the world of the organs and glands and emotions of humankind.

By reading various Scogna-authored books, the Reader is encouraged to discover his or her own awareness level and then learn to increase that level. We understand that it is through self–knowledge that we grow; it is through self-awareness that we can bring about balance in our lives.

This balance and harmony in our own lives will create a ripple that will positively impact all mankind.

We are electrical, spiritual beings of light, and have been set adrift on the seas of life without a handbook to guide us...until now.

Finally, we have a handbook of our human systems for clarity and understanding!

We are so glad you have found us - Welcome!

—Kathy M. Scogna
Summer, 2015
www.KathyScogna.com

A Quick Tour, or How to Use this Book

For all Readers, note that personal health and well-being is our own responsibility; always has been, always will be. But what do you do if you can't see the problem, or worse, what do you do if you don't know the cause of your problems? Because it is in finding those causes, the reasons why, that we can truly find resolution.

If you are not yet working with an SAF practitioner, decide which of your systems are the most agitated, then find those in this book and read about the SAF holistic perspective of these.

With the SAF Method, there is a way for us to find our reasons and causes, and thus to get a better grip on the results, our symptoms. The personal efficacy we gain allows for beneficial change. When we overcome our obstacles, whether small and simple, or large emotional, traumatic stumbling blocks, understanding floods in, we greatly enhance our own life and that of our loved ones, and can better access and utilize our mental telepathic powers.

If working with an SAF practitioner, you can now be an active participant and discover what your line-up of symptoms and emotions mean. You'll understand up close and personal how events in the past have influenced you and your behavior in the present time. Once given the opportunity to see your problems in a new light, something magical will happen. A spark of understanding occurs, energy is released, and the path becomes clear. "*A-Ha!*" you will exclaim; "*now I get it!*"

In SAF, we like to say you'll learn to face your dragons, You can develop more fully your own self determinism.

Now, let's get right to it with some frequently asked questions about SAF!

FAQs

What is SAF?
S.A.F. stands for Self Awareness Formulas. It is a precise method for increasing your self-awareness about your life, your business, your body, your health, your emotions, and your past. SAF was created in the 1980s by Joseph R. Scogna. Jr., who could see the big picture: he cross-connected bio-energetics, psychology, Western medicine, Eastern philosophies, quantum physics, sound and vibration with mathematics and made it into a very workable model.

The SAF method has been used in practitioner's offices ever since. It is now being read in 80 countries!

"Everything is energy."

SAF is a practical use of Energy Medicine.

What can SAF do for me?
SAF can quickly pinpoint a core issue, with specifics.

SAF can identify what physical or emotional situations occurred in the past and have resulted in the core issue, including the approximate age patterns began.

In the future, you may find yourself in a similar situation (realistically, we can't avoid all situations!) but this time, after some SAF work, you'll be more aware and stronger. You'll be able to say, "Hey, wait a minute, this isn't working for me anymore." "Been there, done that." You'll have spotted a behavior pattern **before** it becomes a problem.

How does it work?
Special Questionnaires are used for evaluation and input. We use the Stress-120 for emotional issues, the SAF-120 for physical issues, and the Q-24 for a faster evaluation. If unsure, use the Stress-120. The special Questionnaires are available at your practitioner's office, or your practitioner may opt to send you one by mail. We also use

Infrared and log temperature values at organ venting sites, similar to Chinese and Asian meridian work. This would be done in an office setting with a practitioner who has a special infrared device.

Is the Questionnaire a psychology test?
No; and because it is about you and your own issues, there are no right or wrong answers. It is designed to help you learn about your stressors so you can make positive changes. Like all sciences, SAF® has its own language and special terms.

What is the SAF language?
It is a body-mind-emotion-spirit language and is accomplished by assigning **numbers** to certain organs and glands. Emotions, conditions and various aspects are included. It is the Rosetta Stone for the body, and has already been coded into humans, an ancient-future "speak" you can learn. Much of that coded language is presented in this book. (see Chart on pages 70-71.) More in-depth reading includes *SAF Simplified* and *Junk DNA: Unlocking the Hidden Secrets of Your DNA* (Scogna & Scogna).

Our protein structures (our organs and glands) hold recordings in our DNA of what has happened to us in the past. Everything is recorded—the good, the bad, the ugly! When we identify which organs and glands are stressed the most, this tells us what emotions and other aspects need to be examined.

Emotions are made of energy; these are electrical. Emotions are mental experiences with biochemical (physical) actions, and they dictate to us how to be, how to feel. With SAF chain sequence work, we can pinpoint the connections right down to a certain year. And you will feel instant relief as the stuck emotion is unstuck and released - "A-ha! Now I get it!"

Because it uses numbers, is SAF numerology?
Numerology means "a study of numbers". SAF is not numerology as found in the Bible or new age versions. But

numbers are a universal language. 0 and 1 are the binary language of computers and cell phones and so the use of numbers fits in handily with computer work and SAF.

There is an actual numerical degradation order for our organs and glands, caused by radiation from many sources; this can be read about in *SAF Simplified* and *Junk DNA*. And by the way, Symbols & Mathematics is a sense perception (#113), highlighted in *Junk DNA* as one of the 128 sensory channels.

How does SAF find what organs are stressed?

Using Questionnaires or Infrared generates a string of numbers. This book will tell you what those numbers represent.

Your practitioner will explain that every chain (number sequence) has a story to tell. After transposing it into a grammatical sentence we can learn to read it like a book. The chain presents a snapshot, a slice of life of your personal issue or trauma or whatever block you are working on.

This is not like a birth chart or astrology that can be completed once or twice in a lifetime. Think of an SAF chain as finding a single moment of impact in your life. How many impacts have there been? We humans each embody many, many chains because we've had impacts, injuries, physical and emotional upsets throughout our lives.

If something was in the past, can't I just blot it out? Why do I have to look at it again?

Your body and mind record everything. The pleasant events are light and airy, while the unpleasant ones are compressed energy, and contain heavy emotions, such as anger, hate, fear and grief. Through this awareness method, you'll learn how events in the past are still influencing you, especially the negative emotions of anger, hate, fear and grief.

You'll learn how those early events, many from childhood, gave you an unconscious "code to act," a script that you still follow now, even though consciously, in the present time, you might not want to act that way!

Can you tell me more about the codes?
In our lifetime, and through inheritance of our genetic line, we developed certain survival mechanisms and behavior patterns that helped us cope with life from the time we were helpless children. As we matured, those early life codes, the emotions and actions we created that helped us in the past, may have become obsolete. As an adult, these codes are often no longer workable and what's even worse, these may be **unknown** to us. It is as if a script was written, a record or CD of it continually runs in the background of our mind, directing us, and we are its puppet. Some codes and scripts are good for us, such as, "don't touch the hot stove!" It can be a fun exercise to find others we are following that are no longer so pro-survival for us.

Instead of living life to the fullest, we may find ourselves in situations that are bad for us; in a rut with no way out, or living a life without happiness or joy or purpose. It is important to find the codes and scripts that are mis-directing us, re-evaluate these and edit those that are no longer helpful.

What are some examples of codes and scripts?
You might be following a script to:
- Give in too easily
- Find it hard to say no
- Feel like a failure
- Be dependent or child-like in adult relationships
- Always try to please family
- Do things for others and never do for yourself
- Stifle your expressions (hold it all in)
- Not speak up unless asked
- Be sickly, or have risky behaviors
- Crave or need attention (act out inappropriately)

While these codes and scripts might have worked for a child trying to survive in an adult world, it is easy to see that these can be detrimental for an adult trying to forge healthy relationships.

Who would want to use SAF?
Anyone who envisions a better life! If given the choice, each of us has a problem or two we could do without. It might be a physical or emotional pain or upset, a situation with our family, at work with the boss, or our children, or a pattern that seems to crop up from time to time.
The fact is we DO have a choice. We make choices every day. But somehow we seem to make the wrong choice and our life never improves, or the same old problems pop up time and again.
SAF is for anyone who wants to "seize the day" and make a difference in their life. Are you someone with allergies? Do you seems to have "wars" with drugs or alcohol, foods, people, insects, or animals? SAF is helpful for those who are overly sensitive to civilization and radiant energies of cell phones or emotions, or someone who has recurring traumatic memories from long ago, memories that are still haunting. Or there may be a vague uneasiness about decisions or direction in life.
Again, SAF is not something that is done TO us but is a method in which we are active participants so that our self efficacy will rise. Depending upon your practitioner's area of expertise, you can learn to connect the causes and effects, receive special nutrition, acupuncture or other programs for health, or resolve present day situations by putting past events truly *in the past* where they belong.

Know Thyself!
"Know thyself" is often uttered, but many times is unheeded. In SAF we are interested in increasing our self-knowledge through two environments:
1. the inner workings of our personal holistic systems
2. the exterior connection with our physical environment (our friends and loved ones, business partners, neighborhoods, the electromagnetics around us, the Earth, space and beyond).

How can I get started?
Read *The Numbers of SAF*, the starting point. Decide

which of your systems are the most agitated, then find those in this book and read the SAF holistic perspective of these.

For SAF session work, there are two ways to begin.

1. IN OFFICE:
Ask your practitioner for an Infrared scan and he or she will provide this service. Or ask for a special SAF Questionnaire. Think of a complaint (what you want to work on) and complete an SAF Questionnaire. Return your completed Questionnaire to the practitioner's office and schedule a time for a chain interpretation.

2. REMOTE LOCATION:
Ask your practitioner to mail or email you an SAF Questionnaire. Think of a complaint (what you want to work on) and complete the Questionnaire, then return it to the practitioner's office and schedule a time for a chain interpretation, which can be done in office or by phone.

Using this book:
Ask your practitioner to supply you with the chain sequence of numbers that resulted from your Questionnaire or Infrared. Until your scheduled appointment for an interpretation, you can read about your string of numbers in *The Numbers of SAF*. Although you won't learn how to read a chain in this book, you will be a more educated and interested participant, and your personal work will progress that much faster.

NOTE to the Reader: The SAF program incorporates many sources of information; however, it does not diagnose a condition as in the Western medical model. Remember, your practitioner is there to help you in understanding your holistic system and in helping you find balance and harmony.

SAF By the Numbers

1: Thymus Gland (Immune System, Tonsils, Adenoids, Peyer's Patches & Appendix)

> **At a Glance:**
> Condition: Protection
> Emotion: Aggression
> Low Emotion: Reaction
> High Emotion: Action

Condition / Purpose: Protection

The purpose and function of the #1 system is protection. Throughout time, the number one killer of mankind has been infections and diseases caused by germs and microbes. This #1 system is our first line of defense against infection. There is a war being fought every microsecond between the forces of the body and the forces of the environment. Is the body winning? The answer is contingent upon the strength of the immune system.

The connection between the two physical manifestations, infection and inflammation, is eternal. The invasion of the body (by infection) triggers the immunological response necessary, which induces inflammation and heat (calor) for the destruction of unwanted micro-organisms. The resulting effect is pain (dolor), redness (rubar), and swelling (tumor).

Note that all the components listed above have a necessary use in our fight against invading organisms.

Shock, trauma, and injury predispose us to certain illnesses that require courageous actions on the part of our bodily defense mechanisms. Tumors, swellings, pain and redness are necessary reactions during the battles fought within the body. These occurrences are healing processes.

It is important to note that these symptom reactions can also occur from a mental stance.

Emotion: Aggression
When the #1 system is out of balance, the person may have problems of a mental nature with which he hasn't made connections. He may have a rigid stance and is likely to fall apart when confronted directly. Because the mental aspects affect the physical aspects, with #1, a person will have much stress in life, health, business and family.

Energetically, this system is the **Protector**; it works on an invisible level as an electronic shield, and examines bacterial and toxic frequencies that enter its realm to decide if these should be eviscerated. This system fosters ideas of safety and protection and depends on our ability to deliver just the right amount of aggressiveness at the right time, in order to protect us from outside invading forces.

This #1 system is stimulated and programmed by memories and thoughts of having to endure feeling unsafe and unprotected, in order to survive what we could not change or escape at the time.

Some Expressions: Protective shields are down. Electronic shield has weakened. Fighting off an invading energy. Feelings of aggression; there may be aggression toward us or toward another, or we may feel aggressive toward someone or something. Feeling overwhelmed, without protection. Time to put up your dukes for protection.

We have been reacting to stimulus, our buttons have been pushed, or we are constantly fighting off a cold or negative patterns. With SAF work we learn the history and the pattern, and can go into action, without reacting.

2. Heart & Cardiovascular System

> **At a Glance:**
> Condition: Synchronize
> Emotion: Love
> Low Emotion: Deny
> High Emotion: Accept

Condition / Purpose: Synchronize
The heart is a small pump that extends its energies throughout the entire body; its purpose is to synchronize and keep the system in good running order.

The heart has a most resilient crust but it is up against so much stress and degradation during a lifetime that it succumbs to the easy actions of heart-oriented toxins. Heart disease remains the number two killer of mankind.

The condition of cardiac dysfunction results from heart irregularities getting their start from electro-physical disturbances such as stress, pollution and toxemia. Those who complain of physical heart traumas (actual heart pains and problems, bypass surgery, clogged arteries, etc.) invariably complain of difficulty in their love lives.

Emotion: Love
This #2 system is the **Synchronizer**; it specifically hints at a person's problems with synchronization, meaning that he or she is not able to coordinate the basic activities properly. It is important for the mind to remain organized. When confusion sets into the mind, diseases may run rampant.

Energetically, this #2 system is a love, harmony and synchronization system, and shows our ability to appropriately choose between harmony and disharmony. If we hope to foster true inner feelings of love, we must look to the synchronization and attunement of the mind and the spirit first. To cure your heart, you must cure your mind. We must be mindful to not deny harmony or not over-accept disharmony into our lives.

This #2 system is stimulated and programmed by memories and reminders of times when we had to endure disharmony in order to survive what could not be changed or escaped from at the time.

Some Expressions: A traumatic incident or issues about love. Feeling unloved or being denied love. Difficulty in handling an incident or issue about love. Something comes in vibrating love (wants to "love you") but is instead interference. Can't synchronize; a broken heart. Heart finds only disharmony. Trying to digest love, but can't digest love. This is a diseased state of love; there is confusion about love. You may have unsynchronized feelings and a life that seems unsynchronized as well.

We have been in denial about love because what we experienced was a disguised and disharmonic form. With SAF work, we can understand and learn to accept and embrace love and harmony into our sphere; then we will experience much synchronicity.

3. Colon & Elimination System

> **At a Glance:**
> Condition: Detoxify
> Emotion: Hate
> Low Emotion: Failed
> High Emotion: Achieve

Condition / Purpose: Detoxify
The function of the colon and elimination system is to detoxify.

With the appearance of #3, there may be an acid condition in the colon, a breeding ground for poison, toxins, parasites, bacteria and viruses. There may be constipation. There may be trouble regulating the peristaltic motion, that undulating current that pushes the final remnants of refuse in the colon toward the anus for expulsion.

Emotion: Hate
A person with a #3 in the chain sequence is filled with hatred (strong dislike) and his mind is jammed up, he can't think straight and he has a narrow viewpoint. It is as if he can only see through a small tunnel or tube, much like the colon.

Energetically, this #3 system is the **Eliminator**; it is concerned with releasing what is no longer nurturing you and what your system hates. It tells of your ability to eliminate toxic energy before your life and body become toxic. We must have the flexibility to like and dislike. We need to be able to get rid of what seems evil and hateful to us.

This #3 system is stimulated and programmed by memories and thoughts of being forced to endure toxic situations, toxic people or toxic ideas that could not be eliminated, changed, or escaped from at the time.

Some Expressions: Issues or feelings about hatred or strong dislike. Can't discard unwanted situations, can't handle being held in, as if contained. Need to be realistic; "call a spade a spade". Hate comes into play so we can push an incident or a person away, far away; however, "it" is stuck inside. Can't get him or her or it out. Trapped in a situation we hate. Can't let go of it.

We have been programmed to fail, to have a narrowed view of life and people, and to be hate-filled about it; with SAF session work we can learn to detoxify and embrace the barriers to achieve our best.

4. Stomach & Digestive System

> **At a Glance:**
> Condition: Digestion
> Emotion: Happy
> Low Emotion: Eaten
> High Emotion: Assimilate

Condition / Purpose: Digestion
The purpose of the #4 system is digestion. Food is broken down mechanically and chemically so it can be absorbed and used for cell metabolism.

With the #4 appearing in the number sequence, there may be acute gastritis, which is inflammation and irritation of the lining of the stomach. This prevents the proper release of digestive enzymes needed to break down proteins to ready them for absorption. Anemia could result because B-12 cannot be efficiently assimilated when this type of condition persists.

Emotion: Happy
Digestion transcends the physical. Humans must be able to take in any energy or substance that enters the system in order to be happy, to utilize the circumstances around him. It can be a mass circumstance (nutrients), energy circumstance (pattern of motion or emotion) or concept circumstance (ideas of someone else). If we were to "swallow an idea" that was too large for us to grasp, we would need to break it down into smaller pieces until we had understanding, until we were able to digest it.

Energetically, this #4 system is the **Digester**; it is focused on nurturance and happiness, and your ability to discern and choose what really nurtures and feeds you, without under-choosing what works, or over-choosing what doesn't. It is important when ingesting food, to not ingest the angry words or energy of another, so keep mealtimes as stress free as possible, or do not eat then.

This system is stimulated and programmed by memories and thoughts of you having to endure being unhappy, or feeling un-nurtured, without being able to change or escape from the situation.

Some Expressions: Issues and feelings about happiness; unhappiness. Unable to digest circumstances, concepts, thoughts or the ideas of others. Can't digest, dissolve and assimilate the experiences and situations in your life on various levels. "I may as well digest it because I can't get rid of it." Rely on others to tell you when you're happy (or not). Trying to digest what caused you to be unhappy. "Can't stomach that." Must work very hard at being happy. "That is distasteful to me."

We have been programmed to be eaten up, consumed by messy situations and events; with SAF session work we can break down foods and ideas and assimilate (embrace) these into our system.

5: Anterior Pituitary & the Sinuses

> **At a Glance:**
> Condition: Coordinate
> Emotion: Observant
> Low Emotion: Controlled
> High Emotion: Master

Condition / Purpose: Coordinate

The anterior pituitary is the frontal portion of the master gland. Its purpose is to direct and coordinate the plans of the genetic mechanism throughout the body, including the thyroid, gonads, adrenal cortex and endocrine glands. All that a person is and looks like (hair and eye color, size, shape, body weight) is overseen by the anterior pituitary.

When the #5 appears, there is a lessening of control. In this situation, the sinuses (chambers of gases) are involved. With high tension and energy stirred up and jammed, there may be an acute contagious viral disease: the flu. Persons predisposed to the flu (those who get it once a year or more) usually harbor large amounts of toxins, which are food for any virus.

Emotion: Observant

We must maintain mental control of our existence in order to realize our ideas and concepts. It is the genetic promise that if we postulate an idea into the genetic programming, that idea will appear in mass form. A wish-come-true mechanism. If our wishes and dreams are not coming true, then we have a coordinating problem, and our ability to observe reality is locked up tight. We are not seeing things for what they are; we cannot program our mind so that we will have a logical ending point. Sometimes the distortion is so great, the light frequency coming in is affected; it curves and bends, causing a need to wear eyeglasses or hearing aids.

Energetically, this #5 system is the **Master Coordi-**

nator, and tells of our ability to coordinate, control and direct our life by applying the right dose of the correct energy system as needed.

This #5 system is stimulated and programmed by memories and thoughts of being controlled by others, or not having appropriate control or direction in situations or events you were not able to change or escape from at the time.

Some Expressions: feeling frozen, confusion. Can't bring ideas into fruition. Rocky relationships. Controlled by others, or feeling the need to control others. There is a loss of power to observe reality as it truly is. Distorted ability to observe reality. If you can't see things clearly, how could you coordinate them? The traumatic event is controlling you, so you've lost control. There is a dulled, distorted perception, overlooking of a situation so you can't see or coordinate it. Altered perception of reality, loss of direction, loss of control to face and handle difficult situations, despair.

We have been controlled by and from many sources; with our SAF work, we can identify the causes, realize our wishes, hopes and dreams and become a master of our own life.

6: Liver & Gallbladder

> **At a Glance:**
> Condition: Transmutate
> Emotion: Sadness
> Low Emotion: Aged
> High Emotion: Rejuvenate

Condition / Purpose: Transmutate
The purpose of the liver and gallbladder is to transmutate or change the metabolic processes while digesting fats, proteins and carbohydrates with its enzymes.

The liver takes care of the electro-chemical score tabulated in the blood; it cleanses and adjusts the environment of the whole body by secreting enzymes, and is part of the body's defense system. In short, the liver is responsible for more than 1,000 known functions. Obviously, disruption is harmful to the efficient operation of the entire organism.

The gallbladder holds the bile secretions of the liver until the alkaline compound is ready for use. This important function helps to degrade fat compounds into usable materials.

Emotion: Sadness
Sadness is the opposite of happiness. Unhappy means things are not happening, not going the way we wish to see them. There is a break-up, a split-up, something in the environment is intersecting with the energy. When a short circuit has occurred; the person becomes aged.

Mentally we must be fast enough to keep pace with changes in the environment. If not, the white body light fades and more black body light surrounds us as melancholia, sadness. White body light is visible, while black body light is invisible, which explains why we often cannot see the cause of our depression (it is in the dark and unknown).

Energetically, this #6 system is the **Changer**, it is **Transmutating** or changing what you envision and want into what you actually possess.

This system is stimulated and programmed by memories and thoughts of having to endure traumas of disappointment by giving up on expectations. When you give up on expectations, you are not able to create what you want. Feeling old creeps in; you cannot rejuvenate until you take a look at the past traumas you could not change or escape from at the time.

Some Expressions: Can't transmutate or change the energy you're putting out into what you want to see. Feelings of sadness, great sadness, no hope. Dreams and wishes thwarted. Things are not happening. Old losses are stimulated. Cannot keep or produce what you want.

We have been or feel aged beyond our years by sad circumstances in life; with SAF work we can learn to pinpoint the beginning of the traumatic patterns, change or transmutate our interpretations of these and with that attitude change be rejuvenated

7: Lungs & Respiratory System

> **At a Glance:**
> Condition: Vaporization
> Emotion: Monotony
> Low Emotion: Stifled
> High Emotion: Refresh

Condition / Purpose: Vaporization
　　The overall function of the lungs and respiratory system is vaporization. An exchange takes place: the taking in of fresh gaseous energy and the release of spent gaseous energy.
　　Coughing is an automatic attempt to rid forces invading the respiratory tract. In a case of the common cough (#7), the invaders could have just recently entered the system or could have been there for some time. In the latter case, paroxysms of coughing are chain reactions caused by the infiltration crisis.

Emotion: Monotony
　　#7 is an energy system; it is an invisible process, for the lungs operate on a mass-less level; the lungs are a gaseous detoxifier. It is monotonous, so when the #7 is found in a chain sequence, it indicates this is an often repeated situation.

　　Energetically, the #7 system is the **Exchanger**; it is concerned about breathing with inspiration, which allows resolution and refreshment.
　　This #7 system is stimulated by memories and thoughts of feeling stifled, which happened again and again, and from which you could not let go, process, or escape at the time.

　　Some Expressions: Feelings of being stuck in a routine or a rut. Happens again and again. Can't deal with the invisible, can't process toxins. Feel tired, with breathing problems. Not noticing invisibilities all around. Monotony = chronic = humdrum. Oh no, here it comes again. Invisibility is spread all around your body; it facilitates getting into you, like a gas, like smoke. Could this feeling be the cause or instigation for smoking? Chronic/monotonous seems to pervade everything in life.

We have been stifled in certain situations and were almost unable to breathe; with SAF work, we can now learn to find the cause, take a deep breath as we discharge energies, and be refreshed.

8: Sex Organs

> **At a Glance:**
> Condition: Reproduce
> Emotion: Apathy
> Low Emotion: Separated
> High Emotion: Create

Condition / Purpose: Reproduce

The purpose of the sex organs is to reproduce, to create offspring (children), however, this action of reproducing is found on many levels and aspects of life and living.

The arteries and veins act as corridors and hallways for the life-giving plasma and serum, essential to life and creativity. The person finds this #8 number sequence when the blood vessels of the lower extremities may already be subject to damage and lessened circulation. This affects the sex organs, but the entire system as well; power may be low, the muscles lax, or the tone of body slack.

Emotion: Apathy

The ability to create is first and foremost found in #8; the ability to create any creation - art, music, writing, architecture, children, etc.

In sexual activity, there is a power that comes from the mind. Sexual creativity comes from the ability of a person to intersect his ideas into other subjects or problems so that he can pull out the essential ideas and then can reproduce his own thoughts.

Energetically, this #8 system is the **Connector**; it explains your ability to attract positive relationships and creativity. This system is a measure of your connections with everything and everyone else. Your connections are what you (as Spirit) really want.

This #8 system is stimulated and programmed by memories and thoughts of not feeling safe to trust connections with those around you. You had to endure and survive relationships with apathy, all the while not connecting with your own truth.

Some Expressions: Can't create; major creative cycles have been thwarted. There is a creative block and apathy about it. Issues of a sexual nature, sexual relations, children and family issues. A situation is not blossoming, not reproducing. Feel hopeless or useless about the issue. "I should just give in, give up". "It doesn't matter anymore...." When weakened by apathy, an entity of any sort can gain entrance, and wants to reproduce. Power is low; having difficulties.

We have survived with apathy by telling ourselves we were separate, separated; in our SAF session work we are able to brighten our outlook and reconnect emotionally, and then create what it is we hold most dear.

9. Bones & Muscles

> **At a Glance:**
> Condition: Locomotion
> Emotion: Pain
> Low Emotion: Blamed
> High Emotion: Respond

Condition / Purpose: Locomotion
The function of the bones and muscles is how we can move, our locomotion throughout the day and a lifetime.
In the body, the #9 system denotes the movement of flowing poisons. From the Greek, rheumatism means to "flow like a stream" and gout translated means "to drop". The Greeks believed that the latter condition was created by "drops" of poison within the system – how accurate! Uric acid moves (rheumatism) through the muscles and the joints, and drops its deposit of poison (gout) to create pain, deformity and progressive paralysis.

Emotion: Pain
Pain tells us there is something encroaching, an invader, something that does not belong. It is added pressure – can be known or unknown, conscious or unconscious and it must be detoxified (released).
We can prioritize but with the #9, this tells us that ability is not active. We cannot respond appropriately to straighten out the confusions and put in order; something extra is there, interfering.
We hold onto anguish and many emotions in our bones and muscles. We may blame ourselves and this is hidden in the bones and muscles, too. If resentment is held onto, watch for arthritis.

Energetically, this #9 system is about **Movement**: moving away from painful situations and toward what is fulfilling.
This #9 system is stimulated and programmed by

memories and thoughts of you having to endure painful events or situations that could not be changed or escaped from, even by moving away. We bring it all with us through time!

Some Expressions: Feeling of pain, feeling of poisons moving through. "I can't move, can't prioritize." Can't extricate from a certain problem, the pain source. Mobility is inhibited. Pain is a friend, a warning, to tell you to handle its source. With pain, there is stopped, inhibited or limited motion. Frozen in pain. Mental pain. Discomfort = pain. Held in thoughts, cause pain. "Don't let me feel the pain. Let me move away from it. I can push the pain signals away."

We have held ourselves responsible (or been blamed by others) for conditions not of our choosing. With SAF session work, we are able to let go of the hidden thoughts we are holding onto in our bones and muscles that caused us such pain, and can then respond appropriately.

10: Thyroid (& Veins & Arteries of the Upper Extremities)

> **At a Glance:**
> Condition: Metabolization
> Emotion: Anxiety
> Low Emotion: Criminal
> High Emotion: Justice

Condition / Purpose: Metabolization
The overall purpose of the thyroid is metabolization of the human system. There is a delicate balance being maintained between pressures that are too great or too weak; the thyroid is the monitor of the carbon-nitrogen equation and a radiation monitor as well.
Trouble on this sensory level will result when the random motion of the environment is overwhelming. In this case, the action may be too slow (dizziness) or too fast (vertigo), such as with a hyperthyroid. With hypothyroid, there may be less energy, lowered intelligence and an inclination toward obesity or weight problems. In either situation, which can vacillate on a daily basis, there is a non-optimum effect on the thyroid gland that regulates metabolism of foods and cellular metabolism.
The thyroid can work effectively on physical and mental levels, and so combinations with other systems help to achieve the genetic program of the body.

Emotion: Anxiety
The thyroid can foresee and supervise necessary changes. With the presence of #10, there is a rigid mental stance, ideas may be stuck together, and thoughts of the future may set in motion much anxiety.

Energetically, this system is the **Corrector**; it should be correcting what is not right for you. It affects your ability to know for certain and choose what is right for you. If the wrong choice is made, this #10 will lead the way to take decisive action clearly and quickly to correct what is not right.

This #10 system is stimulated and programmed by memories and thoughts of anxiety, of enduring personal injustice from people, places or things that were not the right frequency for you, and from which you could not process it out, change it, or escape from it at the time.

Some Expressions: Feelings of anxiety. Difficult time with change. Past plans have gone awry, ideas are stuck. A situation seems criminal to you and doesn't allow you to take action that will result in a sense of justice. #10 is a stress organ system, which deals with metabolization, creation and utilization of energy. Anxiety about the future – goals, dreams and desires seem uncertain, unsure. Thoughts of the unknown future cause you to be dizzy, unsteady.

We have been operating under false pretenses in that we were seen as wrong, even criminal; with SAF session work, we can throw off that yoke of anxiety and realize the justice we seek in the correct action.

11: Veins & Arteries

> **At a Glance:**
> Condition: Circulation
> Emotion: Resentment
> Low Emotion: Gravity
> High Emotion: Games

Condition / Purpose: Circulation

The ultimate function of the veins and arteries is circulation; a complex network of tubes allows for the blood to flow on its intended journey and thus #11 is considered an extension of the heart. Principally in the lower extremities, there may be dilated or bulging veins caused by excesses of pressure on the liver, spleen, lymph, bone and heart. The consumption of concentrated starches and sugars contribute to the problem of varicose veins and can aggravate inherited varicosity conditions.

When the #11 appears, this indicates there is a breakdown in circulation somewhere. With mental connections in the chain, such as with the #14 (mind), the person may be focused on other peoples problems, not his own, and so is mentally scattered. With physical connections in the chain sequence, such as with #22 (parathyroid) there may be a predisposition to solidification, spinal misalignment, sciatica, low back troubles, or decaying of teeth and bones.

Emotion: Resentment

Actions taken in the past caused deep-seated resentments. By focusing on these time and again, more of the same are pulled in, to add to the tally. These are not hidden from sight but are well known, harbored and "cared for," full of energy. This is a sensitive person who focuses on others and their problems, and absorbs these, making them his own problems. He will worry about them. #11 in a chain sequence says this is a chronic condition.

Energetically, this #11 system is the **Circulator,** helping us to move and participate in the life we have created, without enduring unnecessary restriction.

This #11 system is stimulated and programmed by memories and thoughts of enduring resentments, which serve to pull us downward just as gravity does; we have participated in very serious and heavy, grave situations and events that could not be processed, changed or escaped from at the time.

Some Expressions: Feelings of resentment, deep-seated resentment, the same traumas and patterns keep repeating. Brooding over real or imagined injuries from the past, "what people did to me." Constant dwelling on the past, thus re-creating past events and situations; this results in feeling scattered. Focused on other people's problems. Can't move as much as before; gravity holds us back.

We have been unable to move as we've wanted, filled as we are with resentments and restrictions from serious and grave events in the past. With SAF work and journaling, we are able to release the restrictions and can once more enjoy the lightness of games we created in our life.

12: Brain & Nervous System

> **At a Glance:**
> Condition: Electricity
> Emotion: Nervous
> Low Emotion: Complicated
> High Emotion: Simplify

Condition / Purpose: Electricity
This #12 system utilizes electricity in its core of operation for the holistic human being on body, mind and spirit levels. At times, there may be excess electrical energy coursing through the nervous system − enough to fry it. There is hyper motion and excitability of the nerves due to high electric stimulation from the environment. This sensing could be received from people, places, things and events that happened at some point in time.

With a #12, there may be headaches, neuralgia, nervousness, which could be biochemical, in which calcium and magnesium are out of balance, or it could arise from mental conflicts.

Depending upon the connections with other organs and glands, there may be food allergies, insomnia, and lack of REM sleep.

Emotion: Nervous
When a #12 appears in the chain sequence, there is attention focused on the unknown, hidden energy, beyond the reach of the person. Not understanding it, not seeing it, causes nervousness. Likewise, unfinished projects and plans cause nervousness.

Energetically, this #12 system is considered the **Simplifier**, in which the flow of energy defuses confusion and complicated situations.

This #12 system is stimulated and programmed by memories and thoughts of enduring complicated and confusing situations. Because you could not process, change or escape from those early situations, feelings of nervousness abound.

Some Expressions: Great nervousness. Attention may be focused on complicated issues. This #12 system is the bridge between known and unknown. Is there an unknown condition? Is it mysterious and dark? You may think your brain is rattled, which leaves you confused.

When we are in the middle of very complicated and entangled situations, filled with electricity, we cannot prioritize what to do first for resolution. With SAF work, we can untangle and unravel those situations to glimpse the value of simplicity, and can begin making simple, clear and uncomplicated choices.

13: Adrenal Glands

> **At a Glance:**
> Condition: Capacitance
> Emotion: Courage
> Low Emotion: Shame
> High Emotion: Pride

Condition / Purpose: Capacitance
The purpose of the adrenal glands is to store electrical charge (energy), this is called capacitance. With this #13 system appearing in the chain sequence, we find the opposite of energy: low blood sugar or hypoglycemia, caused by environmental factors. The person with a #13 in their chain sequence may be losing energy to environmental parasites and thieves. What are these? Radiation (frequency transmissions) of radio, microwaves, TV, computers, x-ray, the sun, and nuclear isotopes. Even emotional radiation from those we love can sap our strength. These all steal energy (glucose or sugar) from a body and replace it with hardened fat and calcium and other inert materials that reduce the efficiency of the overall human mechanism.

Emotion: Courage
With #13, there is a lack of energy. We cannot be courageous when the zest for life and living is diminished. The hypoglycemic may have inert heavy metals, emotional "drainers" (relatives, friends and other energy leaches), plus the company of parasites which take energy. These factors are robber barons that abscond with the most precious substance a human body has - glucose ($C_6 H_{12} O_6$).

Energetically, this #13 system is about **Pressure**, equalizing the pressures of life. When we are able to courageously meet pressure with equal pressure for balance, we can resolve conflicts and regain our self-esteem.
 This #13 system is stimulated and programmed by

memories and thoughts of you having to put up with loss of power, overpowering feelings of not being able to live up to or measure up to expectations (shame), which could not be changed or escaped from at the time.

Some Expressions: Feel emotionally drained; energy thief in the environment; someone or something is taking your energy. You can't handle stress or defend yourself. Feel like running away? The zest for life is dimmed or gone. Without reserve energy, do you turn to coffee or stimulants? No courage to take action; can't fight or run away. Always look nearby for another person who drains the energy, or a traumatizing incident or accident that seemed to be a defining moment.

We have been knuckled under by the pressures of life so that our fight or flight mechanism could not work properly when we needed it to. With SAF work, we are now able to stand tall with pride and can put away the shame or self-expectations we thought we didn't measure up to as we courageously explore our new lease on life filled with energy and new abilities.

14. Mind

> **At a Glance:**
> Condition: Analyze
> Emotion: Wonder
> Low Emotion: Unknown
> High Emotion: Serenity

Condition / Purpose: Analyze
The overall program of the mind is to analyze all data. It is considered in the science of SAF to be an electromagnetic aura that pervades every cell and nuclei of the body, by using command centers around the brain. Paintings by the old Masters depicted the saints and martyrs with very bright golden halos, which show these spirits possessed the most harmony and balance. In contrast, the person with a #14 in their number sequence is a worried person, who constantly mentally computes and ponders their troubles, with no solution in sight. Overanalyzing is a condition of worry.

The mind seems to cup the brain and the skull and stores tiny microfine energies of various wavelengths. The shorter wavelengths register the deep past (connections to genetic philosophies handed down by remote ancestry via the DNA-RNA). The longer wavelengths register a period closer to the present time. It is interesting to note that homeopathic remedies that have incredible diminution (very short wavelengths), can often pull those long ago memories into the present time. The wavelength of a past remembrance is brought forward from ancestral times when energy is pumped into it.

The physical relationship of the body to the mind induces the psychosomatic condition. Because the mind is wired into the main impeller (a junction where physical matter, electricity and psychic power meet), the mind easily causes the motor and sensory areas of the brain to function either properly or improperly.

When under deep stress, the mind has the ability to

create physical reactions, such as headaches. A migraine headache (#14), with nausea and vomiting, can act as a pressure gauge for the surroundings that may include friends, relatives, business associates, etc. and could signal a time for retreat. There could be "a sick feeling" that relates to the person's ability to stand up against environmental pressures

Emotion: Wonder

A person with a #14 in the chain sequence has his attention focused squarely on curious speculations and upsetting subjects. The imagination may be running wild. There could be a good deal of fantasy in play, in which he thinks he has some physical condition when he does not.

There may be fear of confrontations with other disoriented people because the sporadic impingements of the disoriented ones cannot be warded off.

Energetically, this #14 system is the **Analyzer**. It is certainly the analyzer of events and situations in the past in order to predict and create the future, based upon the decisions made in the present time. Here we find the ability to figure out problems with imaginative, effective and creative solutions, in which we change the unknowns into recognizable knowns and thus achieve serenity and balance in our life.

This #14 system is stimulated and programmed by memories and thoughts of worry and wonder over just about everything that has not been figured out ahead of time. It is a condition, not just a passing endeavor. The wonder and worry is not a single thought but a way of life. Therefore, the presence of #14 says there is no way to process, change or escape from this situation.

Some Expressions: Feelings of worry or bewilderment, disagreement. Chronic, constant worry. Mental disturbances. The imagination is filled with wonder and runs wild, leaving no time or ability to analyze or evaluate a situation. Worry and wonder about unknown factors, none of which sinks in or computes. Not the solitary act of thinking but obsession with worry; a worry wort.

We have been wondering and thinking and pondering on unknown subjects for so long, it is as if we are lost in space with no reliable answers in sight. With SAF work, we are able to realize the futility of focusing on the unknown, and instead, we turn our attention to what we do know and what is concrete, which affords us the serenity we desire.

15: Hypothalamus & the Senses

> **At a Glance:**
> Condition: Evaluation
> Emotion: Attention
> Low Emotion: Inhibited
> High Emotion: Communication

Condition / Purpose: Evaluation

The function of the hypothalamus and the senses is evaluation of all the information being presented to us. All outside information comes through to us this way. The hypothalamus is directly associated with the complete balance of the human body during which it accurately regulates heat and cold, appetite, and sex drive. It controls the ability of the human being to discern stress and patterns of pressure on each sense level, which includes sight, sound, smell, taste and touch, but also the complete 128 sense perceptions as detailed in *Junk DNA: Unlocking the Hidden Secrets of Your DNA*.

Can we evaluate situations realistically and put the proper events in perspective? Can we process all the sensory input into a view that clearly reflects an accurate perception of the outside world around us?

When we see the #15 in a chain sequence, the evaluation process is hampered. There may be degenerative conditions created by excesses of radiation, radiant energies and stress. This may be emotional stress, poor dietary habits, from an injury or impact, or nuclear fallout and power plant effluence. #15 tells of problems caused when an individual collides with another energy source.

Emotion: Attention

The appearance of #15 in a chain sequence shows there have been repeated distortions of perception, and an inability to focus our attention for long periods. This trouble stems from simple and complicated forms of energy, any energy from ANY source in the environment (nuclear, electronic smog, smoking haze, people, places, inanimate objects, and emotions from others as emotional radiation) that is directed toward us. Any form of stress and pressure to the system is counted and must be defended against. Any time we have to kick back against pressure, we can be misdirected.

Energetically, the #15 system is the **Communicator**. It is born from the spiritual and interpersonal relationships with higher energies and the Supreme Power (God), who possesses and controls more white body light than any other being. It is part of humankind's quest to emulate God, which makes it imperative that we put our attention on gaining as much white body light as possible. We do this in SAF by locating those areas that are "in the dark," unknown to us, and by bringing those into the light so we can understand it. As the black body light changes to white body light (from invisible to visible), it explodes! Previous unknown emotions and events turn into known occurrences; the mysteries become solved riddles. Along with the newly understood past events are huge bursts of energy, a gift to both client-participant and practitioner.

This #15 system is stimulated and programmed by memories and thoughts of feeling inhibited from communicating what you see, hear and feel in situations that you were not able to process, change or escape from at the time.

Some Expressions: Feelings of overwhelming pressure or stress, degenerative conditions created by too much pressure or stress. Sensory overload, too much information is coming in. Can't discern it, and can't evaluate it. Distracted – can't focus, short attention span. Your radar (#15) must be able to control your attention and put it where you want. Distorted perceptions. Difficult to recall events and emotions. Senses seem to pull in more radiation, more stress. Radiation stress is food for senses. Don't want to look at something. Can't face the issue or the person. Can't say or explain how you feel.

We have been in situations where the sensory input from various frequencies was so great it overwhelmed us, inhibiting words or comprehension. With SAF work, we learn to break into that cycle by evaluating patterns and past events, freeing up our attention units, and with new-found understanding and energy, we can forthrightly communicate to ourselves, to others, and via the written word.

16: Kidneys & Bladder

> **At a Glance:**
> Condition: Filtration
> Emotion: Fear
> Low Emotion: Poisoned
> High Emotion: Purify

Condition / Purpose: Filtration
The overall function of the kidneys and bladder is filtration — filtering and disposing of the cellular debris end-products of body metabolism and other toxins that have gotten into the body. Urine, the refuse of cell debris, is sent to the bladder for storage until voided.
On a physical level, #16 explains that there are kidney and bladder issues.

Emotion: Fear
The #16 system tells of an inability to face, filter and purify toxic emotional situations from your life. There may be fears, phobias and terrors, which can lead to a great deal of pain and sensation. A fear reaction is human energy that is desperately trying to escape from an environmental, physical or mental danger. What happens in the mental realm stimulates the physical. When severely frightened, a primal human reaction is to urinate, to let it go.

Energetically, #16 is the **Purifier** of the holistic human system, so the system will work continuously and seamlessly.
This #16 system is stimulated and programmed by memories and thoughts of enduring fearful feelings and toxic emotional situations in the past that you could not process, change or escape from at the time.

Some Expressions: Feelings of fear. Acute or chronic fear. Terror. Fear of confrontation. Unwillingness to face certain issues. "Is this really going to happen or should I stop my negative thoughts?" Fear of fear. Trying to filter out the good from the bad. Too much urination or too little urination. Keeps toxins or loses nutrition through dumping. Breakdown in filtering process.

We could not face emotionally-charged events without terror gripping our innards, as if poisoned by the negative thoughts flung in our direction. With our SAF work, we now recognize toxic situations when we see them on body, mind and spirit levels, and can take steps for filtering and purifying our life.

17/18. Endocrine System

> **At a Glance:**
> Condition: Equalize
> Emotion: Conservative
> Low Emotion: Perverted
> High Emotion: Balance

Condition / Purpose: Equalize
The overall purpose of the endocrine system is to coordinate all hormonal structures and provide a means to equalize pressure. This endocrine or hormone system consists of the pineal, pituitary, thyroid, parathyroid, thymus, adrenal, pancreas, and ovaries (F) or testes (M).

In the study of SAF, #17/18 is considered the power train of the human system; it creates structure and sequences of energy that cause us to look and behave the way we do. In a certain way, the remaining organs of the human system are merely servomechanisms of this power train.

The presence of #17/18 in a chain sequence of numbers shows that something is awry or upset within the entire hormonal system. Something drastic has happened to change everything.

Two numbers are always used with this system.

17 = pressure = hot and represents the male system.

18 = space or loss = cold/cool and represents the female system.

Emotion: Conservative
This system must be balanced so we can produce power. When there are energy failures, there is a trauma lurking about that needs our attention. When someone is very conserving of their emotional output and can't seem to fulfill their capabilities or potential, or if someone is reluctant to move forward in an endeavor, suspect and look for a trauma to address.

Energetically, this #17/18 system is the **Balancer**. The endocrine system is what helps us achieve and maintain electromagnetic balance. When we see a #17/18, we know the chain owner has lost the balance or perception for the basic dichotomies of life. We can regain homeostasis (balance) on our own by consciously being able to extricate ourselves from certain traumatic patterns, instead of staying in these, out of habit. The trick is to find the traumas and know what to do; this is accomplished with SAF methods.

PLEASE NOTE that with SAF, we are not able to delete a trauma or traumatic event from our memory banks. Because it happened, the event is still a full color image and it may become much clearer, however, by doing awareness work, we can reduce the power, the electrical energy this trauma held over us for so long. We can effectively move the event from black body light into white body light (from the unknown into the known realm) and receive that burst of renewed energy it once held back.

For all energies to remain in harmony, there must be balance and coordination; the reward is power, strength and illumination.

The #17/18 system is stimulated and programmed by memories and thoughts of having to endure some type of perverted or unbalanced trauma situation with no way out, which you could not change or escape from at the time.

Some Expressions: A traumatic event happened in the past and is now stimulated in the mind; it is active. Energy failure, not enough power. Feeling of being unbalanced, uncoordinated. Hormone imbalances. Things seem unequal. The other person has the upper hand. If you get your hand slapped every time you reach for the cookies, you back off and conserve your actions and especially your emotions. There is less of an emotional outlay. Lost balance. Can't perform at fullest capabilities. When male hormones are prominent there is pressure. When female hormones are prominent, there is loss. "If I lose my traumas, I will lose my life" and so we hang on much too long. We tried to forget a terrible event because it was so against our grain, so perverted, so disharmonic that we will put out less energy for its resolution, conserving our emotions for another day, another battle. With SAF work, we learn to identify traumatic patterns and emotions that are no longer helpful, and are no longer as huge as they once appeared, and we can happily and easily extricate ourselves from the pattern and its influence to find our higher balance.

19: Skin

> **At a Glance:**
> Condition: Demarcate
> Emotion: Boredom
> Low Emotion: Lost
> High Emotion: Win

Condition / Purpose: Demarcate

The purpose and function of the skin is to provide a border, to demarcate the limits and edges of the body. It is a solid crystalline shield that is harmonic with the invisible protective shield of the thymus (#1).

With #19 appearing, the home forces have a difficult time fending off attacks by the invader forces of the body. There could be skin reactions, rashes, pimples, psoriasis, This number alludes to boundary violations, such as with emotional radiation or abuse, violence or sexual trespass. It deals with the problem of protection by the largest organ, the skin.

Emotion: Boredom

The skin is a protective covering. The word *boredom* is from Old English and Latin, meaning *to pierce, to bore into*, as with an auger, which may become dull as a result. Energies and even people from the environment are able to bore into us and we then lose our protective covering.

Energetically, this #19 system, the skin, is considered the **Identifier**. #19 appears because we need to increase our ability to define and defend our borders and boundaries. We find with #19, the possibility of a psychic invasion or any boundary violation that has gone beyond the border of the skin. This is sometimes expressed as "he got under my skin" or "that made my skin crawl."

This #19 system is stimulated and programmed by memories and thoughts of feeling you had lost, you had been invaded, your boundaries were violated and you were not able to defend yourself in the past, nor could you change or escape from the situation at the time.

Some Expressions: Diminished protection against invaders. Challenges to established boundaries. "He got under my skin." Overwhelmed, from opposing energies. Deep set chronic disillusionments. Bored feelings, hardened feelings about present day circumstances. Defines borders, invaded boundaries. Your illusions were squashed by the desires of others. Constant violation of boundaries. Someone is encroaching on your space. Out of touch with things, or too much touch. "That made my skin crawl."

We could not defend our boundaries in the past, which triggered a "feeling lost" pattern to replicate on body, mind and spirit levels. With SAF work, we are able to symbolically push away and release the offending violator, and in so doing can revive the exuberant feeling of being found, of winning, much like catching the gold ring.

20: Pancreas & Solar Plexus

> **At a Glance:**
> Condition: Location
> Emotion: Laughter
> Low Emotion: Suppressed
> High Emotion: Express

Condition / Purpose: Location

The overall purpose of the pancreas is for balance; we depend on this complex for balance of body, mind and spirit. When the #20 is found in a chain sequence, it shows we have lost the ability to locate ourselves.

Location problems on the mental plane result from events and traumas that occurred in certain locations on the planet where we used to be. All identifiers and images of location, such as grass, rocks, trees, buildings, cars, atmosphere, sights and sounds, are recorded in the DNA-RNA. Being as transient as we are today, we move on to other areas and often lose the ability to track the energies to the present surroundings, and so there could be homesickness and depression with a #20. The quality of our life has changed.

There may be "lost" organs that we left behind in our travels through life. "I left my heart in San Francisco" is a well-known tune that exemplifies this concept.

The pancreas is loaded with enzymes for the digestion of fats, minerals and sugars. It sustains the equilibrium of energy in the body by controlling the sugar balance with the hormones glucagon and insulin.

The #20 tells of disharmony (low or high blood sugar), which is usually an acute condition with feelings of imbalance, shakiness.

The solar plexus is the nerve center; it balances the nervous system and is directly connected to the earth's center of gravity. As babies, we learned to maintain stability from this centering point. No matter how we are pushed and shoved, we can regain our balance by observing the connection between our solar plexus and the earth's solar plexus, the epicenter of the earth. With help from the pancreas, we are centered in electrical charges of a positive and negative nature (pH = acid-basic balance).

Emotion: Laughter
Laughter is part of the solar plexus mechanism of discharging unwanted energies (toxins). When the solar plexus (#20) is suppressed, we are not in balance.
What is the mechanism of laughter? When we see someone fall and hurt himself, we laugh because we are replaying our own trauma. A connection to the dark recesses has been touched upon and brought into the light. Something has come to the senses that used to be invisible.
It is a part of the life continuum that mind energy, in connection with spiritual energy, produces a magnetic and electric attraction for toxins in the environment. If we are loaded with poisons, any type of poisonous frequency, these were brought in because of a behavioral pattern of ours that acted much like an antenna in the body to attract these poisons.
The trick is to be able to discover and discharge these frequencies. Each type of laugh has a distinctive way of discharging. To be effective at discharging toxins, laughter must be precise. If we twitter, giggle, snicker, laugh from the throat or nose, it will not be effective. We must express our laughter in the proper way, from the solar plexus, beneath the diaphragm, a deep and full belly laugh. Then we will have an effective, electrical discharge laugh.

Energetically, this #20 system is the **Expresser**.
The #20 system is stimulated and programmed by memories and thoughts of you needing to suppress your true feelings and thoughts, in order to feel safe in situations you could not change or escape from at the time.

Some Expressions: Feel weak, off balance, can't regain balance. Center of gravity is off. Can't direct energies in the body. "Where am I?" Laughter discharges toxins, but there is difficulty laughing. It is too serious to laugh off. Don't like where I am now. Latitude and longitude traumatized, stuck programming in a location. Traumatically connected to a place. "I left my heart in ....." Feeling depressed or homesick. A sharp increase of power, followed by a sudden decrease.

When we move to a different location we leave a bit of ourselves behind and shut down the emotions of the past situation. With SAF session work, we are able to shed the shackles of suppression and learn to express our feelings and ideas in creative ways. Laughing off irritants comes easier with this work.

21: Posterior Pituitary (fluid balance)

> **At a Glance:**
> Condition: Hydrolyze
> Emotion: Grief
> Low Emotion: Stuck
> High Emotion: Free

Condition / Purpose: Hydrolyze
The posterior pituitary controls the quantity of water secretions of the system, the hydrolyzation. Lying directly behind the anterior pituitary, the posterior pituitary releases lactating hormones and milk production, releases the unfertilized egg from the ovary, and releases antidiuretic hormones when needed to control the overall fluid balance.

When the #21 appears, there is difficulty controlling water balance; there may be not enough, and so edema ensues as the body tries to adjust and hold onto as much fluid as possible. There may be body odor, cold sweat and sweaty palms, due to the rapid release of toxins through the skin.

Emotion: Grief
Great losses have been suffered, in which energy (people, pets, places, businesses, things) have been pulled or yanked away. Because of the loss factor and space, this #21 system has a female bent. Losses on the physical side are caused primarily by deficiencies, but when we lose pressure, objects, people and places, we are in the position of having energies that we desperately need being stolen from us.

Our primary loss is the inability to rectify what has happened to us in the past (invisible, black body light) equate it to what is happening to us in the present time (visible, white body light) and predict what will happen to us in the future (invisible, black body light) When we can't rectify these ideas, we lose power.

The more we can connect our past with our present, the more powerful we become for the future. The past is where all the energy patterns (existence patterns) are stored. These energy patterns are what give us power (energy). Nothing else.

Energetically, this #21 system is the **Rectifier** between past traumas of loss and feeling stuck in those same images in our present time existence.

This #21 system is stimulated and programmed by memories and thoughts of feeling stuck in losses, not feeling secure in the family setting, or not being your authentic self in past situations that you could not change or escape from at the time.

Some Expressions: Feeling of grief or loss. Tearful. Flooded with tears, emotions, feelings. Feet or ankles swollen, the fluid balance is off. Great losses. Stuck feelings, emotions shut down. Feel degraded when energy (people, places, businesses) have been pulled away from you. Loss of dreams. Can't rectify the past with the present; no future to be seen. Can't make connections. Feel disconnected. Loss of tears.

Many losses over a lifetime cannot be processed without feeling stuck in the middle of it, lost in time. With SAF work we examine the stuck feelings of grief, which makes these lighter in weight, and the resulting energy that is now ours is enlightening and freeing.

22: Parathyroid (calcium balance)

> **At a Glance:**
> Condition: Experience
> Emotion: Anger
> Low Emotion: Solid
> High Emotion: Dissect

Condition / Purpose: Experience.
The function of the parathyroid glands is to regulate the calcium in our cells and tissues and in the blood stream. When we have experiences, we create and release more calcium.

This SAF link #22 indicates the effects that calcium depletion has on the body. Here we find hyperactivity, the state of being in which the person has lost control to be at rest, or cannot easily accept a situation.

Emotion: Anger
Few realize that becoming angry with a person or pressing negative energy towards another causes particles of your own energies to breach their mental skin and this endows that person with MORE energy and power to oppose you. The solution is not to deny the anger, as that would just stuff it downward further into the darkness, but instead to work with it in the SAF method and bring it into the light so the charge of it (the energy) can be released.

With this view, it is nonsensical to create any situation that is of an attack nature. Any kind of aggression serves only to feed the other side.

Energetically, this #22 system is the **Dissector**. We pull things, thoughts or concepts apart so we can see how they work. It is the opposite of becoming more solid, in which ridges of energy encase ideas and proclaim that we are not in a mode to accept....anything.

#22 is stimulated and programmed by memories and

thoughts of feeling anger, of being forced to do or have what you did not want, in situations that you could not change or escape from at the time.

Some Expressions: Feeling of anger, or "I have no anger toward anyone." Hold all anger inside. So heavy, it is cast in stone. Fixed viewpoint, and not willing to change it. Look from one side, one viewpoint only. Not flexible. Things feel solid and rigid. Tears things apart.

In order to survive, we learned to hold our anger in, or push it out toward another person. With SAF work, we learn to identify the anger, dissect it to make it less solid, and finally to fully embrace it as a part of our electrical, emotional experience.

23: Spleen

> **At a Glance:**
> Condition: Rejection
> Emotion: Antagonize
> Low Emotion: Regret
> High Emotion: Appreciate

Condition / Purpose: Rejection

The purpose of the spleen is to hold and process old and worn out blood cells and erythrocytes. It sets hemoglobin free, produces lymphocytes and plasma cells and creates new erythrocytes for fetal life and newborns.

When the #23 appears, there are most likely allergic substances present, and the spleen is the natural organ to gather, reject and eject those.

In an allergy situation, the body thrusts itself away and tries to cast off the offending substances. It does this with wet and running eyes, nose, and ears; with vomiting; a wet or wracking cough; or diarrhea with mucus, all necessitated by the action of pushing off the energy to which the body is sensitive or allergic.

Although allergy is the polar opposite of addiction, we are often addicted to substances to which we are allergic.

Emotion: Antagonize

This #23 explains that the person likes to tease others, which can be irritating. It is comic relief, a way of releasing the chronic feeling of antagonism the person carries around with him. As a result, he could be having a difficult time developing emotional patterns and relationships that are of a higher and more positive note.

In an SAF chain sequence, all those numbers to the left of #23 in the number line up tell where the allergy can be found; and what system is being affected.

There can also be mental allergies; we can be allergic to love or a loved one! (2-23).

Energetically, this #23 system is the **Rejecter**, as it rejects the substances (people, places, things) that are antagonizing, to which the chain owner is sensitive or allergic.

Our inability to reject causes the buildup of the emotional state of hate, which is why it is so important to learn to find, accept and release the energy of past events and traumas. Having a clean holistic view is what brings us harmony and balance.

This #23 system is stimulated and programmed by memories and thoughts of having to survive feelings of rejection in situations you could not change or escape from at the time.

We can easily reject ideas, programs, plans and even our own purpose and goals -- mistakenly. It is the project of SAF to re-acquaint people to their purposes and their plans for life.

Some Expressions: Feeling of rejection, feel rejected. Chronic antagonism. Thorn in the side, a stone in the shoe. Rejection is pushing away. Difficulty developing relationships of a positive note. #23 = Allergy. An allergy = trying to throw off an offending source. "I have an allergic reaction to _____." Can't cope with environment. Mental allergies = "I rejected someone or I have been rejected."

When we stray from the primary directive for our existence, we are liable to create havoc with our present situation. With SAF work we can acknowledge the dalliance, face the regrets and rejections, and with our new direction firmly in heart and mind, finally feel appreciative and grateful for the release work.

24: Lymph System & Electroplasmic Field (EPF)

> **At a Glance:**
> Condition: Accept
> Emotion: Enthusiasm
> Low Emotion: Mystery
> High Emotion: Understanding

Condition / Purpose: Accept

The overall purpose of the lymph system is to cleanse the body of toxins, especially those in the blood stream. The second system in #24 is the electroplasmic field (EPF), the energy field surrounding all life forms. It is a true balancer of pressure levels. We use this field to increase our powers of perception beyond normal realities. (see *Junk DNA*, sensory perception #106)

The opposite of rejection (SAF #23) is acceptance; when we see the #24 present in the chain sequence, the person is happily, exuberantly willing to accept ANY program brought before him, whether it is good for him or not. The trick is to be able to discern the difference and increase self-control.

Emotion: Enthusiasm

The word enthusiasm comes to us from Latin and early Greek: *entheos* and *enthous*, meaning inspired, possessed. With the enthusiasm of #24 (inspired, possessed), it is natural to have excess electricity coursing through the body. If too much, there might be a need for a "quick fix" to slow it all down.

Where an allergy is a pushing away, addiction is a pulling in, the abnormal craving or need for a substance. This addiction could be any substance or discipline - alcohol, cigarettes, coffee, chocolate, over-the-counter stimulants, drugs, excessive exercise, hypnosis, etc.

In an SAF chain sequence, the numbers to the left of #24 will tell what organ-gland system is being manipulated by the addictive force. (an example is 3-24 = taking a substance (24) that stimulates the colon (3). This is often coffee, or a laxative.)

With #24, we also find shock, trauma and unconsciousness, sometimes from accidents and operations. At those times, when the conscious awareness was greatly reduced, an opportunist may have gained entry and use, such as drugs and OTC medicines, or even suggestive words.

When relatively healthy persons with a #24 are asked if they have taken or took drugs, the reply is "*NO, never!*" And yet, they might have been hospitalized where drugs were used, and now are consuming mega-vitamins, cold pills or arthritis medications (OTC, non-prescription pills), exercising 10 times a day or drinking pots of coffee all day long. "Drug" in SAF is anything that is used for a "quick fix" outside of the willpower of the person. It serves to slow down the excess electricity.

Being spiritual, electrical beings of Light, the drug is the resistance, the drag used to slow things down. It puts extra load on the entire system. Remember, it could be ANY material or discipline used outside of one's own willpower and so a person with the #24 may have over-accepted many programs without thinking.

Energetically, this #24 system is the **De-mystifier**. It shines light on the mystery of the unknowns that plague us. In so doing, we garner greater understanding of life as it is.

This #24 system is stimulated and programmed by memories and thoughts of times when you had to accept what was offered, or you found something that would make the situation palatable in order to survive what could not be changed or escaped from at the time.

Some Expressions: Feeling of unconsciousness, accident, shock, trauma. Being dependent on something. Enthusiastic to accept issue; feel like you must accept it and live with it. Issues of enthusiasm; did you flatly accept the trauma as fact? Enthusiasm or addiction for any material

outside of your will; a quick fix for external stimulus to try to handle something. Need a substance to keep going. Drug = drag on the system. "I use _____ when trying to feel good, to slow it down, or to speed it up."
Surrounded always by a mystery too dark to understand, we couldn't seem to get through the day without a fix, a binge of one sort or another, which instilled a much needed boost of energy, or sense of calmness. With SAF work, we are able to increase our personal efficacy, our strength, our self knowledge. We certainly embrace situations with enthusiasm but we have greater acceptance of life as it is and enjoy waves of understanding with new transmissions of smooth energy.

pages 70-71: The Endocrine Sense Channels (SAF Operative Chart) is the language of SAF or how to Operate in SAF. Origins and full explanation in Junk DNA: Unlocking the Hidden Secrets of Your DNA *(Scogna & Scogna).*

Endocrine Sense Channels

SAF #	Action	Condition	Organ/Gland	Emotion	LowEmotion	HighEmotion
1	Against	Protection	Thymus	Aggression	Reaction	Action
2	Run	Synchronize	Heart	Love	Deny	Accept
3	Contain	Detoxify	Colon	Hate	Failed	Achieve
4	Dissolve	Digestion	Stomach	Happy	Eaten	Assimilate
5	Direct	Coordinate	Anterior Pituitary	Observant	Controlled	Master
6	Keep	Transmutate	Liver	Sadness	Aged	Rejuvenate
7	Exchange	Vaporization	Lungs	Monotony	Stifled	Refresh
8	Attract	Reproduce	Sex organ	Apathy	Separated	Create
9	Hold	Locomotion	Bones/muscles	Pain	Blamed	Respond
10	Action	Metabolization	Thyroid	Anxiety	Criminal	Justice
11	Move	Circulation	Vein/arteries	Resentment	Gravity	Games

(also known as the SAF Operative Chart)

12	Time	Electricity	Brain/nervous system	Nervous	Complicated	Simplify
13	Pressure	Capacitance	Adrenal glands	Courage	Shame	Pride
14	Space	Analyze	Mind	Wonder	Unknown	Serenity
15	Result	Evaluation	Hypothalamus/Senses	Attention	Inhibited	Communicate
16	Refuse	Filtration	Kidneys/bladder	Fear	Poisoned	Purify
17/18	Coordinate	Equalize	Endocrine System	Conservative	Perverted	Balance
19	Push	Demarcate	Skin	Boredom	Lost	Win
20	Quality	Location	Pancreas/solar plexus	Laughter	Suppressed	Express
21	Quantity	Hydrolyze	Posterior Pituitary	Grief	Stuck	Free
22	Have	Experience	Parathyroid	Anger	Solid	Dissect
23	Do	Rejection	Spleen	Antagonize	Regret	Appreciate
24	Be	Accept	Lymph	Enthusiasm	Mystery	Understanding

Suggested Reading

Nutrionics: Introduction to Elemental Pairs
Truths from the ancient world of Elements and Alchemy, combined with the Similars of the healing art of Homeopathy, then infused with the energetics of Light and Energy (quantum physics).
How to achieve balance with the elements!

Junk DNA: Unlocking the Hidden Secrets of Your DNA
Open the pages of this book and unlock the hidden secrets ….. Our DNA contains EVERYTHING we needed to know to survive for the past millennia. Five senses? How about 128 Sensory Channels; perceptions that helped Stone Age man survive, and could enhance our world today. The crystals in our DNA hold all the healing information we need.

Crystals transmit information, we just need to listen and be open to the possibilities.

SAF Simplified
Organs and glands and dragons….. Throughout the book we learn how the mind works, and how unresolved traumas from the past can influence our behavior in the present time. Our organs and glands send us messages we were meant to decode…. are we listening? Here is the theory and language of SAF in easy to understand text.

Project Isis: Fundamentals of Human Electricity
Historical connections to alchemy, Traditional Chinese Medicine, and quantum physics.
Read about human energy in electrical terms (voltage, current, ohms) as this best illustrates the transference of energy and communication among the body systems, as well as between the body (mass), mind (energy) and spirit (concept).
Energy, Frequency, and Vibration!

www.KathyScogna.com

Index

#1, 19
#2, 21
#3, 24
#4, 25
#5, 27
#6, 29
#7, 31
#8, 33
#9, 35
#10, 37
#11, 39
#12, 41
#13, 43
#14, 45
#15, 48
#16, 51
#17/18, 53
#19, 56
#20, 58
#21, 61
#22, 63
#23, 65
#24, 67

128 Sensory channels, 15, 48
2-23, 66
3-24, 67

A
Abdo, Dr. John, 77
Accept love, 21
Accept, 67
Addiction is pulling in, 67
Adrenal glands, 43
Aged, 29
Aggression, 20
Allergic to a loved one, 66
Allergy is pushing away, 67
Analyze, 45
Analyzer system, 46
Anger, 63

Antagonize, 65
Anterior pituitary & the sinuses, 27
Anxiety, 37
Apathy, 33
Appreciate, 65
Aquila, Sandy, back cover
Attention, 48
Attraction for toxins, 58

B
Balance, 53
Balancer system, 54
Becoming angry at another, 63
Black body light, 49, 61
Blamed, 35
Bones & muscles, 35
Boredom, 56
Boundary violation, 56
Brain & nervous system, 41

C
Calcium balance, 63
Calcium depletion, 63
Cannot delete trauma, 54
Can't create, 34
Capacitance, 43
Cause is in the past, 15
Changer system, 29
Circulation, 39
Circulator system, 40
Codes and scripts, 15, 16
Colon & Elimination system, 23
Communication, 48
Communicator system, 49
Complicated, 41
Connect past to present, 61
Connected to a place, 59
Connector system, 33
Conservative, 53
Controlled, 27
Coordinate, 27

Corrector system, 37
Courage, 43
Create, 33
Criminal-justice, 37, 38

D
Delete trauma, 54
Demarcate, 56
De-mystifier system, 68
Deny love, 21
Depressed, 59
Detoxify, 23
Digester system, 25
Digestion, 25
Dissect, 63
Dissector system, 63
DNA, 14, 45, 59

E
Efficacy, personal, 11, 17, 69
Electrical beings of light, 68
Electricity, 41
Electromagnetic, 17, 45, 54
Electroplasmic field, 67
Eliminator system, 23
Emotionally-charged, 52
Emotional-mental abuse, 56
Emotions are energy, 14
Endocrine sense channels (chart), 70-71
Endocrine system, 53
Energy thief, 43
Enthusiasm, 67
Equalize, 53
Evaluation, 48
Exchanger system, 31
Experience, 63
Express, 58
Expresser system, 59

F
Face your dragons, 11
FAQs, 13
Fear, 51
Female and male, 53

Fight or flight, 44
Filtration, 51
Find what organs are stressed, 15
Free, 61

G
Games, 39
Getting started with SAF, 17
Gravity, 39
Grief, 61

H
Happy, 25
Happy clients, 76
Hate, 23
Heart & cardiovascular system, 21
High blood sugar, 58
Homeopathy 8
Homesick, 59
Hormone system, 53
How to create a chain, 18
Humors of the Greeks, 8
Hydrolyze, 61
Hypoglycemia, 43, 58
Hypothalamus (& senses), 48

I
I Ching, 7, 8
Identifier system, 56
I left my heart...., 59
Infrared for input, 8, 13-15
Inhibited, 48
Inspired, 67

J
Jerore, Dr. Kathy, 77
Junk DNA, 8, 14, 15, 48, 67, 69, 72
Justice-criminal, 37, 38

K
Kidneys & bladder, 51
Kilian, Brian, 77
Know thyself, 17

L
Language of SAF, 14, 69, 70-71
Laugh (is discharge), 59
Laughing off irritants, 60
Laughter, 58
Liver & gallbladder, 29
Location, 58
Locomotion, 35
Lost our will, 7
Lost, 56
Love & harmony system, 21
Love, 21
Low blood sugar, 43, 58
Lungs & respiratory system, 31
Lymph System, 67

M
Male and female, 53
Manegold, Jim, 77
Master coordinator system, 27
Metabolization, 37
Microscope, invention of, 7
Mind energy-spiritual energy, 58
Mind, 45
Monotony, 31
Movement, 35
Mystery, 67, 69

N
Natural philosophy, 7
Nervous system, 41
Nervous, 41
Numerology, 14
Nutrionics, 8, 72

O
Observant 27
Opposite of rejection, 67

P
Pain, 35
Pancreas, 58
Parathyroid, 63
Perceptions (128), 15, 48, 72
Personal efficacy, 11, 17, 69

Perverted, 53
Poisoned, 51
Porter, Nancy, back cover
Possessed, 67
Posterior pituitary, 61
Practitioners speak, 77
Pressure system, 43
Pride, 43, 44
Project Isis, 8, 72
Protection, 19
Protective shield, 20
Protector system, 20
Psychic invasion, 56
Purifier system, 51

Q
Questionnaires for input, 13, 14, 15, 18
Quick fix, 67
Quick tour, 11

R
Rectifier system, 62
Refreshed, 31
Regret, 65
Rejecter system, 65
Rejection, 65
Rejuvenate, 29
Reproduce, 33
Resentment, 39
Respond, 35
Rosetta Stone, 9, 14

S
Sadness, 29
SAF flashcards, 9, 11
SAF language, 9, 14, 69, 70-71, 72
SAF operative chart, 14, 70-71
SAF Simplified, 9, 14, 15, 72
Self-expectations (shame), 43, 44
Scogna, Joseph R. Jr., 4, 8, 13
Scogna, Nic, 77
Senses, 48
Sensory overload, 49
Separated, 33

Serenity, 45
Sex organs, 33
Sexual trespass, 56
Shame, 43, 44
Shock, trauma, unconsciousness, 68
Simplifier system, 41
Simplify, 41
Sinuses, 27
Skin, 56
Solar plexus, 58
Solid, 63
Something is in the past, 15
Spiritual energy-mind energy, 58
Spleen, 65
Stifled, 31
Stomach & digestive system, 25
Stressed organs, 15
Stuck, 61
Suppressed, 58
Synchronize, 21

T
Tearful, 62

Telepathic, 11
Thymus gland (immune system), 19
Thyroid, 37
Toxic situations, 52
Transmutate, 29
Traumatic event, 55

U
Understanding, 67, 69
Unknown, 45

V
Vaporization, 31
Veins and arteries (thyroid, upper extremities), 37
Veins & arteries (lower extremities), 39

W
White body light, 49, 61
Win, 56
Wonder, 45, 46
Worry, 46

Words from Happy Clients!

Holy Cow! I just finished an SAF session and I feel about 10,000 pounds lighter! Thank you!

"I never realized how defensive I was and how I magnetized so many people into my life that were emotional pollutants for me. After my SAF session, I see them without being defensive, and in the future I'll handle them differently."

"I have a lot more energy since I stopped seeing my situation as such a burden."

"Through chain work, as I prioritize and balance things in life differently, I find I have more balance within myself. This is authentic work!"

"I am now much more aware that my lifetime patterns have been in the genetic pooling. I'm excited that the chains have been broken. And these were long-term issues through several generations! :) "

Practitioners Speak

"This is the Primer we've all been waiting for! SAF yields amazing results and saves hours of time. We can get to the core issues immediately to help resolve traumas and emotional patterns."
—Jim Manegold
james.manegold@gmail.com

"SAF has helped me focus on what I want to create for me, and now I'm doing the same for others. I love the infrared! I work with SAF online almost everyday to find Homeopathics and Bach remedies for my clients."
—Kathy Jerore, ND
inharmony51@hotmail.com

"Joe Scogna's use of infrared is a monumental leap forward in the evaluation of human physiology, psychology, and spirituality. He has given us a unified approach to our holistic health status—past, present, future."
—Dr John Abdo,
DrJohnAbdo.com

"SAF has come full circle. I can collect chain data at expos and shows, enter the information through my phone and I can give instant relief for my clients!"
—Nic Scogna
astermassage@gmail.com

"SAF is quick and easy to use, an extremely advanced technology for personal change and for helping others. The Up-Links in the Interpretations create a comprehensive picture of the ages when traumas occurred, where in the body they are located, and how these are impacting our lives in the present."
—Brian Kilian
bkilian@BellSouth.net

Printed in Great Britain
by Amazon